NIGHTCLUB
SECURITY

HANDBOOK FOR OWNERS AND STAFF

TOM SOTIS

Nightclub Security: Handbook for owners and Staff

© 2024 Thomas Sotis. All rights reserved.

ISNB # 978-1-300-94496-6

Imprint: Lulu.com

To my good friend

David Wilson

Contents

PART 1: The Benefits of Proper Training

Enhanced Safety and Prevention of Incidents

Nightclub security plays a pivotal role in maintaining a safe environment and preventing incidents before they escalate. A proactive approach to risk reduction is key. Well-trained security personnel can identify potential threats early, such as recognizing signs of intoxication, aggression, or suspicious behavior. By intervening promptly, security staff can prevent serious incidents like fights, thefts, or accidents, which reduces the risk of injury to patrons and staff as well as minimizing property damage. This foresight and swift action help create a safer and more enjoyable experience for everyone in the venue.

Crowd control is another critical aspect of nightclub security. Overcrowding can lead to dangerous situations like stampedes or suffocation, especially in high-energy environments. Properly trained security staff are equipped to manage the flow of patrons entering and exiting the venue, ensuring that maximum capacity limits are observed and emergency exits remain accessible. This management prevents bottlenecks and ensures that patrons can move freely and safely throughout the nightclub. By maintaining order and managing crowds effectively, security teams not only prevent accidents but also help the nightclub operate smoothly without unnecessary disruptions.

In summary, enhanced safety and prevention of incidents in nightclubs depend on vigilant, well-trained security teams who can spot potential risks early, manage crowds effectively, and de-escalate situations before they become hazardous. Their proactive efforts create a secure and controlled environment where patrons can enjoy themselves safely.

Improved Customer Experience

The professionalism of nightclub security personnel plays a vital role in enhancing the overall customer experience. Security staff who are trained not only in conflict de-escalation but also in customer service create a welcoming and safe environment for patrons. When guests feel that security is present but not overly aggressive, they are more likely to feel comfortable and enjoy their time. This balanced approach to security helps build trust with patrons, which leads to repeat business and positive word-of-mouth, both of which are essential for the nightclub's long-term success.

Handling intoxicated patrons is one of the most frequent challenges in nightclub security, and how it's managed directly impacts the experience of all guests. Well-trained security personnel know how to de-escalate situations involving intoxicated individuals calmly and professionally, without resorting to unnecessary force or causing public embarrassment. This approach not only prevents situations from escalating but also ensures that the atmosphere remains enjoyable for other patrons. When intoxicated individuals are managed discreetly and respectfully, the overall environment of the nightclub remains pleasant, allowing others to continue enjoying their night without disruption.

In summary, improved customer experience in nightclubs hinges on the professionalism and tact of security personnel. By balancing strong protective measures with excellent customer service, security teams ensure that patrons feel safe, respected, and free to enjoy their time, contributing to a positive and welcoming atmosphere that enhances the club's reputation.

Legal and Liability Protection

Nightclubs face significant legal risks if security personnel are not properly trained in handling incidents. A well-trained security team, educated on the appropriate use of force and how to de-escalate altercations, can significantly reduce the likelihood of lawsuits or legal complications arising from improper actions. For example, following local laws regarding age verification and alcohol service ensures that the nightclub avoids hefty fines or legal actions related to serving minors. By adhering to these legal standards, security personnel protect both themselves and the nightclub from unnecessary legal exposure.

Compliance with safety regulations is another key element in legal and liability protection. Security personnel who understand fire codes, occupancy limits, and crowd control best practices help ensure that the nightclub operates within the law. Failure to comply with these regulations can result in fines, penalties, or even the temporary closure of the venue. Therefore, well-trained security staff who monitor capacity limits and keep exits clear are critical for maintaining regulatory compliance, thus safeguarding the business against potential financial and legal penalties.

Incident documentation is also an essential component of legal and liability protection. When incidents occur, accurate and timely reporting by security personnel can serve as vital evidence in legal disputes or insurance claims. A detailed report documenting the incident, the individuals involved, and the actions taken by security staff can help protect the nightclub from lawsuits and prove compliance with legal protocols. Proper incident documentation ensures that the nightclub has a clear, defensible record if any legal challenges arise.

In conclusion, effective training and legal compliance in nightclub security reduce legal risks, ensure regulatory adherence, and provide valuable protection in the event of lawsuits or claims.

Reputation Management

Reputation is a vital asset for any nightclub, and the presence of professional and competent security personnel plays a significant role in shaping public perception. A nightclub with well-trained security staff is viewed as a safer and more inviting place for patrons to enjoy themselves. Guests are more likely to feel comfortable knowing that security is visible but non-intrusive, and that any conflicts will be handled efficiently and respectfully. This positive atmosphere attracts more customers and can lead to repeat business, driving higher revenues and establishing the nightclub as a reputable venue in the community.

Effective security also helps a nightclub avoid negative publicity, which can have lasting consequences on its reputation. Incidents such as fights, altercations, or accidents are sometimes inevitable, but how they are handled can make all the difference. A nightclub with trained security personnel who know how to de-escalate situations, enforce rules fairly, and respond to emergencies with professionalism is less likely to face negative headlines or bad press. Conversely, poor handling of incidents—such as excessive use of force, failure to follow legal protocols, or mishandling of intoxicated patrons—can quickly lead to damaging media coverage that tarnishes the nightclub's image.

In a highly competitive industry, maintaining a good reputation is crucial. Patrons are more likely to frequent venues where they feel safe and respected. Through proper security training and ongoing professionalism, nightclubs can foster a positive public image, encouraging more visitors and ensuring long-term success while avoiding the negative impact of bad press or legal fallout from mishandled incidents.

Increased Profitability

Effective nightclub security contributes directly to increased profitability by enhancing the overall guest experience, attracting high-profile clientele, and protecting the venue from costly damages. High-level security, which prioritizes both safety and discretion, is a significant draw for VIPs, celebrities, and high-profile guests who expect a secure and private environment when enjoying nightlife. When a nightclub is known for providing excellent security, it becomes an attractive destination for high-end clients, leading to lucrative bookings, private events, and higher ticket sales. The presence of VIPs can also enhance the club's reputation, drawing in more patrons eager to share the same space, ultimately boosting revenue.

In addition to attracting high-profile guests, trained security personnel play a critical role in preventing theft, vandalism, and property damage. Nightclubs are susceptible to theft, especially in crowded environments where personal belongings can be targeted. Vandalism and property damage can also occur, whether intentional or as a result of rowdy behavior. Effective security staff can monitor high-traffic areas, intervene when suspicious behavior is detected, and ensure that patrons respect the venue's property. Preventing these issues reduces losses for the owner and helps maintain the nightclub's aesthetic, which is essential for keeping the venue appealing and presentable to future guests.

Furthermore, well-trained security personnel help ensure the smooth operation of the nightclub by managing crowds and resolving conflicts efficiently. When security staff can quickly de-escalate situations or handle disturbances without disrupting the flow of the event, the nightclub can continue operating without interruption. This minimizes downtime and ensures that patrons remain inside, enjoying the experience, thus maximizing sales from tickets, drinks, and other services. Altogether, effective security boosts profitability by protecting the venue, ensuring smooth operations, and attracting high-end clientele.

Retention of Quality Employees

Effective security in nightclubs plays a crucial role in not only protecting patrons but also ensuring the safety of staff members, such as bartenders, waitstaff, and DJs. Nightclub employees often work in a high-energy, sometimes chaotic environment, which can expose them to potential conflicts, unruly patrons, or dangerous situations. When employees feel safe and supported by a well-trained and responsive security team, they are more likely to stay at their jobs for longer periods, which in turn reduces staff turnover. Lower turnover leads to significant cost savings for the business by minimizing the need for constant recruitment, training, and onboarding of new employees.

Additionally, a professional security team contributes to creating a structured and well-regulated work environment. Employees working in a nightclub with strong, visible security feel more confident that any disruptive incidents will be handled efficiently and without escalating into major issues. This sense of security fosters a more positive and professional work atmosphere, where employees can focus on their duties without worrying about their personal safety. A structured, well-regulated environment not only encourages current staff to stay but also attracts quality employees who seek out workplaces where they can thrive without unnecessary stress or fear of unsafe working conditions.

By protecting staff and maintaining a professional environment, nightclubs with effective security are better positioned to retain high-quality employees who are essential to the club's long-term success. Employees who feel valued, safe, and supported are more likely to deliver excellent service to patrons, which in turn enhances the nightclub's reputation and contributes to its overall profitability and growth.

Efficient Handling of Emergencies

Emergency preparedness is a critical component of nightclub security, ensuring that personnel are equipped to respond quickly and effectively to various crises, such as fires, medical emergencies, or violent altercations. Properly trained security staff can assess situations swiftly and take appropriate action to save lives, protect property, and minimize the impact of the emergency. In emergencies like fires, well-trained security personnel can guide patrons to safety through designated exits, help extinguish small fires if possible, and ensure that the evacuation process is orderly and efficient. In medical incidents, trained security can provide immediate first aid or CPR until professional medical assistance arrives, potentially saving lives and reducing the severity of injuries.

Furthermore, security teams must be adept at handling violent altercations or other dangerous situations before they escalate into larger problems. Quick intervention can prevent injuries and keep the nightclub environment safe for other patrons. By anticipating risks and having clear emergency protocols in place, security personnel can contain and manage crises more effectively, limiting damage to both people and property.

Coordination with law enforcement and emergency responders is another vital aspect of efficient emergency management. Security personnel who are trained in working with law enforcement agencies can assist police, paramedics, or firefighters by providing crucial information about the incident, securing the scene, and controlling crowds. This collaboration leads to faster and more efficient resolutions, minimizing disruption to the nightclub and helping operations resume quickly. Additionally, by maintaining clear lines of communication with emergency responders, security teams ensure that critical situations are handled with precision, protecting both patrons and the nightclub's reputation.

In summary, well-prepared security teams can handle emergencies efficiently, mitigating risks and ensuring the safety and continuity of the nightclub's operations.

Minimizing Insurance Costs

A nightclub with well-trained security personnel is not only safer for patrons and staff but can also lead to significant financial savings by minimizing insurance costs. One of the key benefits is the potential for lower insurance premiums. Insurance providers often assess risk factors when determining premiums, and a nightclub with a proactive approach to security is typically seen as a lower-risk establishment. Nightclubs that can demonstrate strong security protocols, such as thorough ID checks, crowd management, and conflict resolution, may qualify for reduced premiums, as insurers recognize the decreased likelihood of incidents like underage drinking, violence, or property damage.

Additionally, effective security measures reduce the number of incidents that lead to insurance claims. Well-trained security staff can prevent or de-escalate conflicts before they escalate into serious issues, such as fights, vandalism, or theft. By maintaining a controlled and secure environment, the nightclub can significantly reduce the frequency of incidents that would otherwise result in costly insurance claims. Fewer claims over time not only contribute to lower immediate insurance costs but can also improve the nightclub's risk profile, leading to further reductions in premiums in the long term.

In summary, investing in professional, well-trained security personnel has a direct impact on minimizing insurance costs for nightclub owners. The combination of lower premiums and reduced claims creates significant savings, allowing nightclub management to allocate resources more efficiently while maintaining a safe and secure environment for patrons and staff. In this way, quality security contributes not only to safety but also to the financial health of the business.

Building Long-Term Success

Effective security is a cornerstone of building long-term success for any nightclub. Trained security personnel play a critical role in ensuring consistent operations by preventing incidents and managing potential issues before they escalate. When security can efficiently handle conflicts, prevent underage entry, and ensure a safe environment, the nightclub can operate without unnecessary disruptions, such as fights, thefts, or property damage. This proactive approach not only helps the club avoid legal complications and fines but also keeps it in good standing with local authorities and regulatory bodies. A nightclub that runs smoothly, without frequent interruptions, is better positioned for sustained growth and long-term profitability.

Additionally, security contributes to the creation of a positive atmosphere where patrons feel safe, comfortable, and eager to return. Repeat business and customer loyalty are essential for the sustainability of a nightclub. When patrons know that the venue prioritizes their safety through visible but non-intrusive security measures, they are more likely to come back and recommend the nightclub to others. This word-of-mouth promotion, driven by positive experiences, helps to build a strong reputation, further attracting new customers and maintaining a steady flow of loyal patrons.

By maintaining safety, minimizing disruptions, and creating a welcoming environment, effective security fosters both short-term success and long-term viability. Nightclubs that prioritize strong security measures are more likely to thrive, with fewer incidents affecting their operations and a solid base of repeat customers ensuring consistent business. In this way, investing in well-trained security is not just about safety—it's about building a foundation for lasting success.

PART 2:

Introduction to Nightclub Security

Nightclub security is a critical component of ensuring the safety and enjoyment of patrons, staff, and performers within nightlife venues. Security personnel are not only responsible for maintaining order but also play a key role in creating an environment that is both welcoming and secure. Given the unique challenges that nightclubs present, from managing large crowds to handling potential conflicts, it is essential for nightclub security staff to be well-trained in various areas. This introduction will cover twelve essential elements of nightclub security that form the foundation of an effective and professional security team.

1. Understanding the Role of Security Personnel

Security personnel in a nightclub setting have a multifaceted role. They are the first line of defense in maintaining order, preventing disruptions, and protecting guests and staff from harm. However, their role extends beyond mere physical presence; they must also act as customer service representatives, helping patrons feel safe and welcomed. A clear understanding of these responsibilities ensures a balanced approach to nightclub security.

2. Legal Knowledge

Security professionals must have a thorough understanding of the laws and regulations that govern nightclub operations, including licensing, alcohol service laws, and the rights of patrons. Knowledge of local and state laws is crucial to avoid liability and ensure that security measures are compliant with legal standards.

3. Effective Communication Skills

Good communication is key to preventing misunderstandings and de-escalating potential conflicts. Security personnel should be trained to communicate clearly, assertively, and respectfully with patrons, staff, and law enforcement. Non-verbal communication, such as body language, also plays an important role in maintaining a secure atmosphere.

4. Access Control and Crowd Management

Controlling access to the venue is one of the most important tasks for nightclub security. This includes checking IDs, managing guest lists, and ensuring that maximum occupancy levels are not exceeded. Proper crowd management techniques help prevent overcrowding and ensure a safe flow of people in and out of the venue.

5. Conflict Resolution and De-escalation

Conflicts are inevitable in any nightclub environment, but how they are handled can mean the difference between a peaceful resolution and a violent escalation. Security personnel should be trained in conflict resolution techniques that focus on de-escalating tense situations before they become physical. This involves staying calm, using verbal strategies, and avoiding the use of force unless absolutely necessary.

6. Physical Security Skills

While the primary goal is to prevent physical confrontations, security staff must be prepared to use physical skills when required. This includes knowing how to restrain individuals without causing injury, as well as understanding basic self-defense techniques.

7. Emergency Procedures

Nightclub security must be well-versed in emergency procedures, including how to respond to fires, medical emergencies, and evacuations. Regular drills and clear communication channels ensure that all staff are prepared to act quickly and effectively in case of an emergency.

8. Surveillance and Monitoring

The ability to monitor activity both inside and outside the venue is critical. Security personnel should be trained to use surveillance equipment and conduct regular patrols to identify potential risks before they escalate.

9. Cultural Sensitivity and Inclusivity

Nightclubs attract diverse crowds, and security personnel must be trained to interact respectfully and appropriately with individuals from different backgrounds. Cultural sensitivity and inclusivity are key to ensuring that all patrons feel safe and welcome.

10. Handling VIP and High-Profile Guests

Security for VIPs and high-profile guests requires a heightened level of discretion and professionalism. These individuals may have special requirements, and security staff must ensure their safety while respecting their privacy and avoiding disruptions to the general crowd.

11. Post-Incident Management

Once an incident has occurred, security staff must document it thoroughly and report it to the appropriate parties. This includes filing incident reports, preserving evidence, and cooperating with law enforcement if necessary.

12. Ongoing Training and Drills

Nightclub security is an ever-evolving field, and ongoing training is essential. Regular drills, workshops, and courses on the latest security techniques and technologies help ensure that personnel are always prepared for new challenges.

By mastering these twelve elements, nightclub security teams can create a safe, enjoyable, and efficient environment for all.

Understanding the Role of Security Personnel

Security personnel play a crucial role in the nightclub environment, where the primary objective is to create a safe and enjoyable space for all patrons. Their responsibilities go far beyond standing at the entrance or patrolling the premises. A successful security team combines physical presence with professionalism, communication skills, and quick decision-making to ensure incidents are prevented and resolved peacefully when they arise. This comprehensive understanding of the role is vital for maintaining order, ensuring compliance with laws, and upholding the reputation of the nightclub.

Overview of Responsibilities

The responsibilities of security personnel in a nightclub are diverse and multifaceted, covering a wide range of tasks that contribute to the overall safety and security of the establishment. Understanding these duties is essential for creating a cohesive and effective security strategy. Below are key responsibilities that every nightclub security professional should understand and master.

1. Crowd Control

Crowd control is one of the most visible aspects of nightclub security. Security personnel are responsible for managing the flow of patrons entering, exiting, and moving around the venue. Nightclubs, especially during peak times, can become overcrowded, increasing the risk of incidents such as fights, accidents, or even stampedes. To prevent these situations, security guards must carefully monitor the number of people allowed in at any given time, ensuring the venue stays within legal capacity limits.

Moreover, inside the venue, security staff must ensure that crowd movement remains orderly. This involves preventing bottlenecks in high-traffic areas like entrances, exits, bars, and restrooms. Crowd control also extends to the dance floor, where excessive rowdiness or pushing and shoving can quickly lead to dangerous situations. By monitoring and managing these spaces effectively, security personnel help maintain an enjoyable environment for all.

2. Access Management

Access management is another critical responsibility. Security guards are tasked with controlling who enters the nightclub, ensuring that only authorized individuals are allowed in. This often involves checking identification to verify the age of patrons and ensuring compliance with any guest list or ticket requirements.

In addition to verifying IDs, access management includes controlling who has access to restricted areas such as VIP sections, employee-only areas, and backstage zones where performers or staff are working. It is essential that security staff manage these areas with precision, maintaining both safety and exclusivity for high-profile guests.

3. Incident Prevention

The best nightclub security teams are proactive rather than reactive. They understand that preventing incidents before they happen is far more effective than dealing with them after they've escalated. Security personnel must constantly be on the lookout for warning signs of potential problems, such as patrons who appear intoxicated, agitated, or aggressive.

By identifying these individuals early on, security can take steps to intervene before a situation spirals out of control. This might involve removing overly intoxicated patrons, calmly speaking with someone who is visibly upset, or closely monitoring individuals who seem prone to aggressive behavior. Through active observation and preventive measures, security personnel help maintain the safety and order of the nightclub.

4. Conflict Resolution

Despite the best efforts at incident prevention, conflicts will inevitably arise in nightclub settings. When tensions flare between patrons—whether it's a misunderstanding, a fight over a spilled drink, or a heated argument—security personnel are the first line of defense in resolving these situations.

Conflict resolution requires a delicate balance of firmness and diplomacy. Security guards must be able to de-escalate tense situations by using verbal strategies, such as calm communication and active listening. They should aim to resolve disputes peacefully, without resorting to physical force unless absolutely necessary. Their ability to stay composed under pressure and find solutions that satisfy all parties is key to maintaining a safe atmosphere in the club.

5. Ensuring a Safe Atmosphere for Patrons

Ultimately, nightclub security personnel are responsible for ensuring that the venue remains a safe place where patrons can enjoy themselves without fear of harm. This involves not only preventing and managing incidents but also fostering a sense of security and comfort. Security staff should be visible and approachable, encouraging patrons to seek their help if needed. By maintaining a strong but friendly presence, security personnel help create a positive atmosphere that enhances the overall nightclub experience.

Professionalism and Image

Security personnel are often the first point of contact for patrons entering a nightclub. As such, they are responsible for setting the tone for the rest of the evening. Their demeanor, appearance, and communication can have a significant impact on how guests perceive the venue, and by extension, how they behave within it. Maintaining professionalism and a positive image is essential for nightclub security to effectively fulfill their role.

1. Projecting Authority

One of the primary functions of security personnel is to establish and maintain authority within the nightclub. However, authority doesn't mean intimidation or aggressive behavior. Rather, it's about projecting a calm, confident, and commanding presence that conveys control without causing unnecessary fear or discomfort.

Security guards should stand tall, maintain eye contact, and speak with clarity and assertiveness. This authoritative presence helps prevent problems before they arise by sending a clear message to patrons that the nightclub is being carefully monitored and that disorderly behavior will not be tolerated.

2. Maintaining Professionalism

Professionalism is essential in every aspect of nightclub security. This includes everything from arriving on time and adhering to the dress code to interacting courteously with patrons, staff, and law enforcement. Security personnel must always maintain a level-headed approach, even in the face of difficult or intoxicated individuals.

Part of professionalism also involves being discreet. Security staff must handle sensitive situations, such as ejecting unruly guests or addressing inappropriate behavior, with as little disruption to other patrons as possible. By maintaining discretion, security can prevent embarrassing situations and ensure that the overall atmosphere of the nightclub remains positive.

3. Approachability and Customer Service

While authority and professionalism are crucial, security personnel must also be approachable. Nightclub security is about more than just maintaining order; it's also about ensuring that guests feel safe and supported. Patrons should feel comfortable approaching security with concerns, whether it's about lost belongings, suspicious behavior, or personal safety.

Security guards can foster approachability by smiling, making friendly eye contact, and being willing to engage in positive interactions with guests. This customer service aspect of security helps build trust between patrons and security staff, creating an environment where people feel secure knowing that assistance is readily available if needed.

4. The Balance Between Firmness and Friendliness

Nightclub security personnel must strike a careful balance between firmness and friendliness. They must be firm enough to enforce rules and prevent problems but friendly enough to foster a welcoming environment. This balance can be challenging, especially when dealing with intoxicated or unruly patrons. However, security guards who master this balance will be able to manage the venue effectively while contributing to a positive nightlife experience for everyone.

Conclusion

Understanding the role of security personnel in nightclubs is essential for creating a safe and enjoyable environment. Their responsibilities range from managing crowds and access control to preventing incidents and resolving conflicts. Professionalism, authority, and approachability are all key components of their role. By mastering these elements, security personnel can not only ensure safety but also contribute to the overall success and reputation of the nightclub. A well-trained and professional security team is indispensable to the smooth operation of any nightlife venue.

Legal Knowledge

Nightclub security personnel must have a strong understanding of the laws and regulations that govern their actions, the nightclub's operations, and the conduct of patrons within the venue. Without this foundational knowledge, security staff may inadvertently violate laws, expose the nightclub to legal liability, or jeopardize the safety of guests. Legal knowledge ensures that security staff can act within the bounds of the law while maintaining a safe and secure environment.

This section will explore the legal aspects of nightclub security, focusing on two key areas: the laws and regulations that security staff must abide by and the importance of licensing and compliance with local and state requirements.

Laws and Regulations

Security personnel in a nightclub must be fully aware of local, state, and federal laws that affect their duties. Some of the most critical areas of legal concern include the use of force, the detainment of individuals, patrons' rights, handling intoxicated or underage individuals, and managing patrons involved with illegal substances.

1. Use of Force

One of the most important legal considerations for nightclub security is the appropriate use of force. Security staff may, at times, need to remove unruly patrons or defuse physical altercations. However, any use of force must be reasonable and proportional to the threat posed by the situation. Excessive force can lead to serious legal consequences, including criminal charges, civil lawsuits, or damage to the nightclub's reputation.

Security personnel should be trained in the legal definitions and limits surrounding the use of force. For example, they must understand the concept of self-defense and the legal thresholds for when force is permissible. Typically, force is justified only when a security staff member or another individual is in immediate danger, and it must stop as soon as the threat is neutralized. The legal principle of "reasonable force" should guide security staff in their actions, meaning that they can only use the minimum amount of force necessary to control the situation.

2. Detainment of Individuals

Another important legal consideration for nightclub security is the detainment of individuals. Security personnel are not law enforcement officers and must operate within the limits of the law when it comes to detaining patrons. In general, security staff do not have the authority to arrest individuals. They can, however, detain someone temporarily if a crime has been committed on the premises, such as theft, assault, or vandalism, but this must be done carefully.

Detaining someone for too long or without proper cause can lead to charges of false imprisonment. To avoid this, security personnel must be trained in when and how they can legally detain individuals. Ideally, security should detain someone only long enough for law enforcement to arrive and take over the situation. The key is to ensure that any detainment is reasonable, necessary, and does not infringe upon the person's rights.

3. Rights of Refusal

Nightclub security personnel have the right to refuse entry or service to individuals who do not comply with the venue's rules or appear to be a potential threat to the safety of others.

However, this must be done in accordance with local laws and anti-discrimination regulations.

For example, refusing entry based on someone's race, gender, sexual orientation, or other protected characteristics is illegal and can result in significant legal repercussions. On the other hand, security can legally refuse entry to patrons who are overly intoxicated, underage, improperly dressed according to club policy, or acting in a disruptive manner. Security staff must be trained in understanding what constitutes a legal reason for refusal, so they can enforce these rules without crossing into discriminatory practices.

4. Handling Minors

Nightclubs are typically adult-only venues, and security staff must strictly enforce age restrictions, particularly when alcohol is being served. Security personnel are responsible for ensuring that no minors gain access to the nightclub or consume alcohol on the premises. Failure to enforce these laws can lead to significant legal issues for both the security staff and the venue, including fines, license suspension, or even criminal charges.

Security staff must be adept at checking identification and verifying the age of all patrons. In some cases, minors may attempt to use fake IDs to gain entry, and security must be trained to recognize these attempts. If a minor is discovered inside the nightclub, it is the responsibility of security to remove them from the premises and take appropriate action to ensure that the law is upheld.

5. Handling Intoxicated Patrons

One of the most common issues nightclub security personnel face is dealing with intoxicated patrons. Serving alcohol comes with significant legal responsibilities, and security staff must be aware of how to handle individuals who are visibly intoxicated. Over-serving alcohol to already-intoxicated patrons is illegal in most jurisdictions, and it is the responsibility of the nightclub and its security staff to prevent this from happening.

Security must be trained to recognize the signs of intoxication and take action to ensure that overly intoxicated individuals do not pose a danger to themselves or others. In many cases, this may involve removing the individual from the premises or arranging for safe transportation home. If an intoxicated individual becomes disruptive or violent, security personnel must know how to manage the situation without escalating it unnecessarily.

6. Handling Illegal Substances

Nightclub security must also be aware of the laws surrounding illegal substances. In many nightlife environments, patrons may attempt to bring illegal drugs into the venue or use them while inside. Security staff must be vigilant in identifying signs of drug use or possession and act within the law to address these issues.

In most cases, security personnel should report illegal drug activity to law enforcement rather than attempting to deal with it themselves. However, they should be prepared to intervene if drug-related behavior puts other patrons at risk. Security must also be familiar with their rights when conducting searches, as unlawful searches can lead to legal challenges.

Licensing and Compliance

In addition to understanding the laws that govern their behavior, nightclub security personnel must also be aware of licensing and compliance requirements. These regulations ensure that the nightclub operates legally and that security staff are properly trained and certified to handle their responsibilities.

1. Security Licenses and Certifications

In many jurisdictions, security personnel must obtain specific licenses or certifications to work in a nightclub setting. These licenses may require background checks, training in the use of force, conflict resolution, first aid, and other relevant areas. Security staff should be fully aware of the licensing requirements in their area and ensure that their certifications are up to date.

Nightclubs may also be required to hire security personnel through licensed agencies or ensure that independent contractors hold the appropriate certifications. Failure to comply with these regulations can result in fines, legal liability, and the potential loss of operating licenses for the venue.

2. Fire Codes and Safety Regulations

Nightclubs must comply with local fire codes and safety regulations, and security personnel play a key role in enforcing these rules. This includes ensuring that maximum occupancy limits are not exceeded, that fire exits remain unobstructed, and that emergency equipment, such as fire extinguishers, is in working order.

Security personnel must be trained to monitor crowd sizes and enforce occupancy limits, as violations of fire codes can lead to significant fines, legal action, or even closure of the venue. In the event of an emergency, security staff must be familiar with the venue's evacuation plan and assist in guiding patrons to safety.

3. Compliance with Alcohol Laws

Nightclubs that serve alcohol are subject to strict regulations regarding alcohol service. Security staff must be aware of these laws, including when to refuse service, how to handle intoxicated individuals, and the rules surrounding alcohol sales to minors. Compliance with these regulations is essential to avoid legal issues and maintain the nightclub's liquor license.

Conclusion

Legal knowledge is an essential aspect of nightclub security. Security personnel must be familiar with laws regarding the use of force, detainment, rights of refusal, and handling intoxicated or underage patrons. In addition, they must ensure that they are properly licensed and that the nightclub complies with local safety regulations, fire codes, and alcohol laws. By staying informed and adhering to these legal requirements, security personnel can protect both the nightclub and its patrons, ensuring a safe and lawful environment for everyone.

Effective Communication Skills

Effective communication is one of the most essential skills for nightclub security personnel. In a high-energy, often chaotic environment, the ability to communicate clearly and professionally can make the difference between a safe, enjoyable night for patrons and one marred by conflict or confusion. Security staff need to know how to interact calmly with intoxicated or difficult individuals, coordinate with teammates, and de-escalate potentially volatile situations, all while maintaining control and professionalism.

This section will focus on three critical areas of communication for nightclub security: verbal de-escalation techniques, interpersonal skills, and team communication.

Verbal De-escalation Techniques

Verbal de-escalation is a powerful tool for security personnel, allowing them to manage conflicts and reduce tensions before they escalate into physical altercations. Nightclubs are high-energy environments where alcohol and large crowds can increase the likelihood of misunderstandings or disagreements. In these situations, the way security staff communicate can often defuse a tense situation without needing to resort to force.

1. Remaining Calm

The first rule of verbal de-escalation is to remain calm. Security personnel are often called into situations where patrons are intoxicated, agitated, or emotional. These situations can quickly escalate if security reacts with aggression or impatience. By staying calm, security staff can project authority and control, which can help defuse the situation.

A calm demeanor starts with controlling body language, facial expressions, and tone of voice. Security staff should avoid appearing tense, angry, or threatening. Instead, they should use open, non-confrontational body language and speak in a steady, calm tone. This approach helps to reassure the patron and signal that the situation is under control.

2. Clear and Direct Communication

When attempting to de-escalate a situation, security personnel should use clear, direct language. Avoiding ambiguity or confusion is essential. For example, instead of saying, "Maybe you should calm down," security personnel should say, "Please calm down so we can sort this out."

Clear communication also involves being concise. In tense situations, patrons may have difficulty processing long, complex instructions. Therefore, it's important to keep messages simple and direct. For example, "Please step outside so we can talk" is much more effective than a lengthy explanation about the rules.

3. Active Listening

Active listening is another crucial component of verbal de-escalation. Often, patrons in conflict just want to be heard, and taking the time to listen can help calm them down. Security staff should let the person express their concerns or frustrations and acknowledge their feelings without interrupting or arguing.

While listening, it's important to maintain eye contact and give verbal or non-verbal cues that indicate attention, such as nodding or saying "I understand" or "I hear you." This helps validate the patron's feelings and shows that security personnel are interested in finding a solution, which can reduce defensiveness and hostility.

4. Offering Solutions and Alternatives

Once the individual has expressed their concerns, security personnel can begin to offer solutions or alternatives. This step involves problem-solving and presenting options that allow the patron to feel like they have some control over the situation.

For example, if a patron is upset about being asked to leave, the security guard might offer, "I understand you're frustrated, but for your safety and everyone else's, we need to ask you to step outside for a moment. We can arrange a safe way for you to get home." By providing options and explaining the rationale behind them, security staff can make patrons feel less cornered and more willing to comply.

Interpersonal Skills

Nightclub security personnel must have strong interpersonal skills to handle a wide range of interactions with patrons, staff, and law enforcement. These skills are not just about maintaining order; they also play a significant role in customer service, ensuring that all patrons feel safe and welcome while adhering to the club's rules and guidelines.

1. Enforcing Rules Without Aggression

Enforcing nightclub rules, such as dress codes, age restrictions, or behavior guidelines, requires tact and diplomacy. Security staff should be firm but polite when addressing rule violations. Instead of making demands or threats, they should explain the reasons for the rules and why they need to be followed.

For example, when addressing a dress code violation, instead of saying, "You can't come in dressed like that," security could say, "I'm sorry, but our dress code requires patrons to wear [specific attire]. I'd be happy to help you figure out how to meet the requirements for entry." This approach makes the patron feel respected and is more likely to lead to a positive outcome.

2. Handling Intoxicated or Difficult Patrons

Dealing with intoxicated patrons is a common and challenging task for nightclub security personnel. These individuals may be uncooperative, belligerent, or disoriented, making communication difficult. However, it's important to approach intoxicated patrons with respect and patience.

Security staff should use calm, non-threatening language and avoid confrontational gestures. The goal is to guide the intoxicated person toward compliance, whether that involves leaving the premises, stopping disruptive behavior, or seeking medical attention. Offering help rather than issuing demands can help avoid resistance. For example, saying, "It looks like you've had a bit too much to drink. Let's get you some water and help you get home safely," is far more effective than, "You're too drunk—get out."

Respectful communication is key to preventing situations from escalating, especially when patrons are intoxicated or emotional.

3. Building Rapport with Patrons and Staff

Security personnel are often seen as authority figures in nightclubs, but they also play an important role in customer service. Building rapport with patrons by greeting them warmly, offering assistance when needed, and maintaining a friendly demeanor can create a positive atmosphere. Patrons are more likely to respond positively to security staff they perceive as approachable and helpful.

Additionally, building strong relationships with other staff members—bartenders, servers, and management—ensures smoother communication and coordination in addressing issues. Good relationships with staff can help security stay informed about potential problems and address them before they escalate.

Team Communication

Nightclub security is rarely an individual task; it requires coordination and communication between team members to ensure safety and order. Effective team communication enables security personnel to respond quickly and efficiently to incidents, manage large crowds, and provide backup when necessary.

1. Radio Communication

Radios are a common tool used by security teams to stay in constant communication. Security staff must be trained on how to use radios effectively, including knowing the appropriate channels for different situations, keeping communication brief and clear, and following protocols for calling for backup or reporting incidents.

In high-pressure situations, effective radio communication can make the difference between a quick resolution and a dangerous escalation. For instance, if a fight breaks out, the first security officer on the scene should quickly radio the team with the exact location and nature of the incident, allowing backup to arrive prepared to assist.

2. Protocols for Calling for Backup

There are situations where a single security guard may not be able to handle a situation alone, such as breaking up a large fight, handling multiple intoxicated patrons, or responding to an emergency. In these cases, calling for backup is essential. Security teams should have clear protocols in place for when and how to call for backup. This helps ensure that situations are handled safely and effectively, minimizing the risk to both security staff and patrons.

For example, protocols might dictate that if a security officer feels threatened, they should immediately radio for assistance and move to a safe position until backup arrives. This allows security teams to approach situations with the appropriate number of personnel to de-escalate without unnecessary risk.

3. Communication During Emergencies

Emergencies, such as fires, medical crises, or violent incidents, require swift and coordinated responses. Security personnel must be trained in emergency communication protocols, including how to coordinate with law enforcement, fire departments, and medical services. Clear communication within the team is essential for evacuating patrons, securing the premises, and assisting first responders.

Security teams should conduct regular drills to practice emergency communication and response, ensuring that in the event of a real emergency, all team members know their roles and responsibilities.

Conclusion

Effective communication skills are crucial for nightclub security personnel, helping them to manage conflicts, interact respectfully with patrons, and coordinate with their team. Verbal de-escalation techniques, such as staying calm, speaking clearly, and actively listening, can prevent situations from escalating into violence. Strong interpersonal skills allow security staff to enforce rules without aggression and build rapport with both patrons and other staff members. Finally, effective team communication ensures that security personnel can work together to maintain safety, respond to incidents, and handle emergencies efficiently. By mastering these communication skills, security teams can create a safer and more enjoyable nightclub experience for all.

Access Control and Crowd Management

Access control and crowd management are among the most critical components of nightclub security. Given the high-energy and often unpredictable environment of nightclubs, maintaining safety while ensuring a smooth, enjoyable experience for patrons requires highly trained and attentive security personnel. Access control and crowd management encompass various elements, such as ID checks, age verification, search procedures, and crowd behavior monitoring, to prevent incidents before they escalate into more significant issues. This guide focuses on essential strategies for effective access control and crowd management in a nightclub setting.

ID Checks and Age Verification

One of the primary responsibilities of nightclub security personnel is preventing underage patrons from entering the venue and consuming alcohol. Strict age verification protocols are necessary to comply with legal requirements and avoid hefty fines or license revocation. Security staff must be proficient in checking identification and spotting fake IDs.

1. Training Staff to Check IDs

Security personnel should be trained to follow a consistent process when checking IDs. This includes asking patrons to present their identification cards clearly, inspecting them for authenticity, and verifying that the patron is of legal drinking age. Guards should take their time, focusing on the key elements of an ID, such as the patron's photo, date of birth, expiration date, and the overall quality of the card.

Training should include an understanding of different types of ID cards (driver's licenses, passports, military IDs) and the variations in their appearance based on the issuing state or country. Staff should also be aware of common features of legitimate IDs, such as holograms, UV markings, and other security features.

2. Spotting Fake IDs

Spotting fake IDs is a critical skill for nightclub security. Fake IDs can range from amateur attempts to highly sophisticated forgeries. Guards should be trained to look for common signs of a fake ID, such as:

- Incorrect font size or type.

- Blurry or altered photographs.

- Mismatched information (e.g., hair color or eye color discrepancies).

- Damaged edges or signs of tampering, like peeling laminate.

- The absence of security features, such as holograms or UV ink.

Security personnel should also be taught to ask follow-up questions when something seems off, such as asking the patron their birth year or address to see if it matches the information on the ID.

3. Legal Considerations

Nightclub security must ensure compliance with local, state, and federal laws regarding alcohol service. In most jurisdictions, serving alcohol to minors is illegal, and nightclubs can face significant penalties for violating this rule. Security staff must ensure that anyone entering the venue is legally permitted to do so. If a patron is found using a fake ID, security should have a clear protocol for denying entry and potentially alerting law enforcement.

Search Procedures

A vital component of access control is ensuring that patrons are not bringing weapons, drugs, or other contraband into the nightclub. Entry screening procedures, including pat-downs, bag checks, and the use of metal detectors, help prevent dangerous items from entering the venue. However, security personnel must be trained to conduct these searches in a manner that respects patrons' rights and privacy.

1. Pat-down Procedures

Pat-downs should be conducted respectfully and professionally to avoid discomfort or conflict with patrons. Staff should clearly explain the procedure before starting and perform the search efficiently. Pat-downs should be same-gender whenever possible to avoid allegations of inappropriate behavior. Guards should be trained to use open hands when searching for weapons or contraband and avoid invasive or unnecessary contact.

If a patron refuses a pat-down, security must know how to handle the situation appropriately, typically by denying entry while calmly explaining the policy.

2. Bag Checks

Many nightclubs require bag checks at the entrance to prevent patrons from bringing in contraband or prohibited items. Security personnel should be trained to check bags thoroughly without invading privacy unnecessarily. They should inspect the main compartments, outer pockets, and any hidden sections where prohibited items could be concealed.

Clear signage at the entrance can help inform patrons about what items are not allowed inside the venue (e.g., weapons, outside alcohol, drugs, etc.), helping to avoid conflicts during the search process.

3. Use of Metal Detectors

Metal detectors, whether handheld or walk-through, are commonly used in nightclubs to detect weapons such as knives or firearms. Security staff must be trained to use this equipment effectively and understand what to do if an alarm is triggered. Clear communication is critical; staff should calmly explain the process to patrons, letting them know what items are not allowed and offering solutions if prohibited items are detected (e.g., storing items in a secured locker or returning them to their vehicle).

4. Legal and Ethical Considerations

Search procedures must be conducted within the bounds of the law. Security personnel should be aware of the legal requirements in their area regarding searches and seizures, including patrons' rights. Overly aggressive or invasive search procedures can lead to legal action or damage the nightclub's reputation. Ensuring that searches are respectful and transparent helps avoid these risks.

Controlling Entry and Exit Points

The smooth management of entrances and exits is vital for maintaining order within a nightclub, especially during busy nights. Security staff must be trained to control the flow of patrons effectively, manage access to VIP areas, and handle crowd movement at closing time, when large numbers of people may be exiting the venue simultaneously.

1. Managing Entrances and Exits

The main entrance and exit points of a nightclub can become crowded, especially during peak hours. Security personnel must regulate the flow of people entering and exiting to avoid bottlenecks, which can lead to frustration, pushing, or even dangerous stampedes.

Staff should be positioned at entrances and exits to monitor the number of people entering and leaving the venue, ensuring that the nightclub does not exceed its maximum occupancy limit. Crowd control barriers can be used to guide patrons into orderly lines, preventing chaotic situations from arising. Security staff should also be aware of fire codes and ensure that exits are always kept clear and accessible.

2. Controlling VIP and Restricted Areas

VIP areas, backstage sections, and employee-only zones require additional levels of access control. Security staff assigned to these areas must verify the identity and authorization of anyone attempting to enter. This may involve checking wristbands, stamps, or names on guest lists.

It's important for security to handle access control to VIP areas with professionalism and discretion. VIP patrons expect a level of exclusivity and protection, so security staff must ensure that unauthorized individuals do not gain access while treating everyone with respect.

3. Handling Crowd Flow at Closing Time

Closing time presents unique challenges, as a large number of patrons may attempt to leave the venue simultaneously. Security staff must manage this situation to prevent overcrowding at exit points, fights, or other disturbances.

One way to manage crowd flow is by gradually encouraging patrons to exit the club as closing time approaches, rather than allowing everyone to leave at once. Security personnel should guide patrons calmly and provide clear instructions to avoid confusion or frustration.

Monitoring Crowd Behavior

Once inside the nightclub, patrons' behavior needs to be closely monitored to identify potential problems before they escalate. Security personnel must be trained to recognize signs of trouble within the crowd, such as overly aggressive behavior, verbal altercations, or signs of excessive intoxication or drug use.

1. Recognizing Signs of Trouble

Security staff must be observant and vigilant, continuously scanning the crowd for any behavior that could indicate a potential problem. Early detection is critical for preventing conflicts from escalating. Signs of trouble can include:

- Verbal arguments that seem to be escalating.

- Patrons who appear overly intoxicated, disoriented, or aggressive.

- Individuals engaging in suspicious behavior, such as frequent trips to secluded areas or unusual interactions with other patrons (e.g., suspected drug deals).

- Groups gathering in ways that could obstruct movement or create friction with others.

2. Dealing with Overly Intoxicated Patrons

Excessive intoxication is one of the most common issues nightclub security faces. Intoxicated patrons may become disruptive, aggressive, or unable to care for themselves. Security staff must know how to handle these situations with patience and professionalism. This often involves calmly removing the individual from the venue, offering assistance with finding transportation, or calling medical help if necessary.

3. Addressing Aggressive Behavior

Aggressive behavior, whether verbal or physical, should be dealt with swiftly to prevent it from escalating into violence. Security staff should intervene at the earliest signs of aggression, using verbal de-escalation techniques to calm the situation. If necessary, they should be prepared to remove individuals from the premises safely and professionally.

Conclusion

Access control and crowd management are crucial components of nightclub security. By effectively managing ID checks, conducting searches, controlling entry and exit points, and monitoring crowd behavior, security personnel can prevent incidents and ensure a safe environment for patrons. Proper training in these areas allows security staff to maintain order, respect patrons' rights, and ensure that the nightclub operates smoothly and safely.

Conflict Resolution and De-escalation

Conflict resolution and de-escalation are essential skills for nightclub security personnel. Nightclubs, with their loud environments, alcohol consumption, and large crowds, are naturally prone to conflicts and disturbances. Security staff are responsible for ensuring the safety of patrons and maintaining a positive atmosphere by managing and resolving conflicts before they escalate into violence or other serious incidents. Proper training in recognizing threats, understanding the balance between verbal and physical de-escalation, and handling intoxicated patrons can significantly reduce the likelihood of dangerous situations occurring.

This section will explore conflict resolution and de-escalation techniques that nightclub security personnel should master to effectively manage potentially volatile situations.

Recognizing Threats Early

The first step in conflict resolution is identifying the potential for conflict before it escalates. Recognizing early signs of aggression, intoxication, or disorderly conduct is essential for preventing small problems from turning into major incidents. Training security personnel to be vigilant and proactive in spotting these early warning signs can make all the difference in maintaining a safe nightclub environment.

1. Signs of Aggression

Aggressive behavior can manifest in many ways, and security personnel must be able to spot it before it becomes physical. Common signs of aggression include raised voices, hostile body language, excessive gesturing, clenched fists, and aggressive eye contact. Patrons who appear agitated or are engaged in heated verbal exchanges with others may also indicate a potential conflict.

Security staff should be trained to observe these behaviors and intervene early, before the situation escalates into a fight or altercation. Early intervention can often be as simple as checking in with the individuals involved, asking if everything is okay, and reminding them of the club's rules regarding acceptable behavior.

2. Identifying Intoxicated Patrons

Intoxicated patrons are among the most common sources of conflict in nightclubs. Alcohol and drug use can impair judgment, lower inhibitions, and lead to aggressive or disruptive behavior. Security personnel must be able to identify patrons who are visibly intoxicated to prevent them from causing harm to themselves or others.

Signs of intoxication include slurred speech, unsteady gait, confusion, excessive sweating, loud or disruptive behavior, and a lack of coordination. Early detection of these signs allows security staff to take preemptive action, such as refusing further alcohol service, removing the patron from the venue, or offering assistance in getting home safely.

3. Recognizing Disorderly Conduct

Disorderly conduct, such as excessive rowdiness, inappropriate behavior, or refusal to follow club rules, can also escalate into more serious conflicts if not addressed quickly. Patrons engaging in disruptive behavior on the dance floor, for example, may accidentally injure others or provoke confrontations. Security staff must monitor the crowd and be ready to intervene when patrons' actions begin to disturb the atmosphere.

Once security personnel recognize these early warning signs, the next step is to engage with the individuals involved and attempt to de-escalate the situation before it worsens.

Physical vs. Verbal De-escalation

Effective conflict resolution requires a balance between verbal and physical de-escalation techniques. Security personnel should prioritize non-physical methods of conflict resolution and only use physical intervention as a last resort. By relying on verbal strategies to defuse situations, security can often resolve conflicts peacefully without the need for force.

1. The Importance of Verbal De-escalation

Verbal de-escalation is the most effective and safest method of conflict resolution. The goal is to calm the situation, reduce tension, and find a peaceful solution without resorting to physical force. Verbal de-escalation techniques include:

- Staying calm: Security personnel should remain calm and composed, even in the face of aggression. Their tone of voice should be calm, clear, and non-confrontational, as this can help defuse the situation.

- Active listening: Listening to the patron's concerns and acknowledging their feelings can help security personnel establish rapport and reduce hostility. Sometimes, people just want to feel heard, and showing empathy can go a long way toward resolving the issue.

- Setting boundaries: Security staff should use clear, direct language to communicate expectations and rules. For example, instead of saying, "You need to calm down," they might say, "Please lower your voice and step over here so we can discuss this."

- Offering solutions: Providing a solution or compromise can help patrons feel like they are part of the resolution process. For instance, offering to escort a patron outside to cool off or suggesting they take a break can help de-escalate a tense situation.

Verbal de-escalation requires patience and practice, but when used effectively, it can prevent situations from escalating to the point where physical intervention is necessary.

2. When Physical Intervention is Necessary

While verbal de-escalation should always be the first approach, there are situations where physical intervention may become necessary. If a patron becomes physically violent, poses an immediate threat to others, or refuses to comply with verbal commands, security staff may need to use force to control the situation. However, physical intervention must be proportionate to the threat and comply with legal standards regarding the use of force.

Security personnel should be trained in restraint techniques that allow them to safely remove individuals from the premises without causing harm. The use of force should always be a last resort, and security must ensure that their actions are reasonable and justified under the circumstances. Excessive force can lead to serious legal consequences, including civil lawsuits and criminal charges.

In situations where physical intervention is required, security staff should work in teams to minimize risk to themselves and others. Coordinating with team members and following protocols for handling aggressive or violent patrons ensures that physical intervention is conducted safely and professionally.

Handling Intoxicated Patrons

Managing intoxicated patrons is one of the most common challenges faced by nightclub security personnel. Alcohol and drug use can lead to a variety of problematic behaviors, including aggression, disorderliness, and impaired decision-making. Security staff must be trained to handle these individuals in a way that minimizes risk and prevents further escalation.

1. Recognizing Signs of Intoxication

As mentioned earlier, security personnel must be able to recognize signs of intoxication early on to prevent issues from arising. Slurred speech, unsteady movement, loud or erratic behavior, and confusion are common indicators of intoxication. Once these signs are identified, security staff should closely monitor the individual and be prepared to intervene if necessary.

2. Escorting Intoxicated Patrons

When dealing with intoxicated patrons, the primary goal is to remove them from the venue safely and without further escalation. Security personnel should use verbal de-escalation techniques to calm the patron and guide them toward the exit. For example, they might say, "I think it's best if we step outside and get you some fresh air." The key is to remain non-confrontational and avoid using force unless absolutely necessary.

If the patron becomes aggressive or refuses to leave, security staff must follow established protocols for physical intervention, ensuring that any force used is proportionate and legal. If the patron is so intoxicated that they cannot care for themselves, security should take additional steps to ensure their safety, such as calling a taxi, contacting friends, or arranging medical assistance.

3. Avoiding Escalation

The most important aspect of handling intoxicated patrons is avoiding escalation. Intoxicated individuals can be unpredictable, and situations can quickly spiral out of control if security responds with aggression or impatience. By maintaining a calm, professional demeanor and using non-threatening language, security personnel can often prevent conflicts from escalating. In cases where a patron is highly intoxicated, providing a clear path for them to leave the premises without embarrassment or confrontation is often the best approach.

4. Legal Considerations

Security personnel must also be aware of the legal responsibilities involved in dealing with intoxicated patrons. Over-serving alcohol to already-intoxicated individuals is illegal in many jurisdictions, and security staff should work closely with bartenders to ensure that patrons are not being served past their limit. Additionally, if a patron becomes a danger to themselves or others, security staff may need to involve law enforcement or medical professionals.

Conclusion

Conflict resolution and de-escalation are critical skills for nightclub security personnel. By recognizing early signs of aggression, intoxication, and disorderly conduct, security staff can intervene before situations escalate into violence or other serious incidents. Verbal de-escalation techniques should be the primary method for resolving conflicts, with physical intervention only being used as a last resort and in accordance with legal standards. Finally, handling intoxicated patrons requires patience, professionalism, and a commitment to ensuring the safety of all individuals involved. By mastering these techniques, nightclub security personnel can maintain a safe and enjoyable environment for everyone.

Emergency Procedures

Nightclub security personnel play a critical role in ensuring the safety of patrons during emergencies. Given the dynamic and often unpredictable nature of nightclubs—where large crowds, loud music, alcohol, and occasionally confrontations are common—security staff must be prepared for a range of potential emergencies, including fires, medical incidents, and violent outbreaks. Proper training and protocols in emergency procedures help ensure that staff can respond swiftly and effectively, protecting patrons and minimizing risks.

This section will explore three key areas of emergency preparedness for nightclub security: evacuation protocols, first aid and medical emergencies, and fire safety.

Evacuation Protocols

In any emergency, the ability to evacuate patrons quickly and safely is of paramount importance. Whether it's a fire, a medical emergency, or a violent outbreak, security personnel must know the correct evacuation procedures to guide patrons out of the nightclub efficiently while maintaining calm.

1. Training in Evacuation Routes

The first step in effective evacuation is ensuring that all security personnel are familiar with the nightclub's layout, including designated evacuation routes. Training should include walkthroughs of the building, identifying all exits, corridors, and areas that could become choke points during an emergency. Security staff should also be aware of alternative routes in case certain exits are blocked or inaccessible.

Regular drills should be conducted to practice evacuation protocols, so that security personnel can confidently guide patrons out of the venue, even under stressful conditions. Nightclubs can be complex environments with multiple floors, rooms, and restricted areas, so it is critical that staff are well-versed in the best routes to guide large crowds to safety.

2. Guiding Patrons to Safety

During an emergency, panic can spread quickly, causing confusion and chaos. Security personnel must be trained to maintain order and calm, as panicking crowds are more likely to cause injuries or create dangerous situations, such as stampedes. Security staff should use clear, authoritative language to instruct patrons, such as "This way, please" or "Follow me to the nearest exit," while remaining calm and composed.

Crowd control techniques, such as forming lines or directing patrons in small groups, can help reduce the risk of overcrowding at exits. Security should also be stationed at key points along the evacuation routes to prevent bottlenecks and ensure that patrons move steadily towards the exits. In the case of patrons with mobility issues or special needs, security should be trained to assist them safely and quickly, ensuring that no one is left behind.

3. Maintaining Calm in Chaotic Situations

The ability to maintain calm during an emergency is crucial for security personnel. Patrons may become confused, fearful, or even aggressive when faced with an unexpected crisis, so security staff must project a sense of control and confidence. Loud, clear instructions and a calm demeanor can help reduce panic and encourage patrons to follow directions. Security personnel should avoid yelling or making sudden movements that could escalate anxiety or confusion among the crowd.

In addition to maintaining calm, security staff should be aware of how to handle individuals who may not cooperate during an evacuation, such as intoxicated or uncooperative patrons. Clear communication and, if necessary, gentle physical guidance can be used to ensure that these individuals leave the premises without causing delays or endangering others.

First Aid and Medical Emergencies

Medical emergencies are not uncommon in nightclubs, where intoxication, physical altercations, and accidental injuries can all occur. Security personnel should be trained in basic first aid, CPR, and the use of Automated External Defibrillators (AEDs) to provide immediate assistance in the event of an injury or medical emergency.

1. First Aid Certification

All nightclub security staff should be certified in basic first aid. This training allows them to provide initial care for common injuries such as cuts, sprains, or head injuries until professional medical help arrives. First aid training also helps security staff manage more serious injuries, such as those resulting from falls, fights, or accidents, minimizing the risk of further harm.

2. CPR and AED Training

Cardiac events, while less common, can still occur in nightclubs, especially in situations involving drug use, extreme alcohol consumption, or physical exertion. Security personnel should be trained in CPR (cardiopulmonary resuscitation) to assist individuals who suffer cardiac arrest. This training should be refreshed regularly, as CPR techniques evolve over time to improve survival outcomes.

The availability and use of AEDs (Automated External Defibrillators) are crucial in saving lives during cardiac emergencies. Security staff must be trained to quickly access and use these devices, as time is of the essence in these situations. AEDs are designed to be user-friendly, but regular practice in their use will help ensure that staff can respond confidently and effectively in the event of a medical emergency.

3. Handling Overdoses and Intoxication

Nightclubs are environments where alcohol and drug use are prevalent, and overdoses or severe intoxication can occur. Security personnel must be trained to recognize the signs of drug overdoses or alcohol poisoning, such as extreme disorientation, unconsciousness, vomiting, or shallow breathing. Quick intervention in these cases is crucial to preventing fatalities or long-term damage.

Security staff should be trained to administer basic care, such as ensuring the individual is breathing, placing them in the recovery position (on their side to prevent choking), and calling emergency services immediately. It's important that security remains calm and takes control of the situation, ensuring the individual receives professional medical help as soon as possible.

Fire Safety and Exits

Fires are one of the most serious potential emergencies in a nightclub setting. The combination of large crowds, dark environments, and flammable materials (such as decorations or alcohol) makes fire safety a top priority. Security personnel must be trained in fire prevention measures, understand how to use fire safety equipment, and ensure that emergency exits remain accessible at all times.

1. Fire Safety Training

Security personnel should receive comprehensive fire safety training that covers how to prevent fires, respond to fire alarms, and guide patrons to safety in the event of a fire. This training should include practical drills, such as using fire extinguishers, recognizing the different classes of fires (electrical, grease, etc.), and knowing how to contain a small fire before it spreads.

Security staff should be trained to conduct regular checks of the venue to ensure that fire hazards, such as blocked exits or overcrowding, are avoided. Ensuring that emergency lighting and signage are in working order is also a critical aspect of fire prevention.

2. Fire Exits and Clear Exit Routes

One of the most important elements of fire safety is ensuring that all emergency exits are clearly marked, accessible, and free from obstructions. Security personnel should regularly inspect exits to ensure they are not blocked by furniture, equipment, or crowds. During busy nights, it is easy for patrons to congregate near exits, unaware that they are creating potential safety hazards.

Security staff should be stationed near fire exits during high-capacity events to ensure that they remain clear and functional. In the event of a fire, these staff members are responsible for guiding patrons toward the exits, ensuring that the evacuation is orderly and that panic is minimized.

3. Fire Drills and Evacuation Planning

Security staff should participate in regular fire drills to practice evacuation procedures. These drills should simulate real-life fire scenarios, allowing staff to rehearse the steps necessary to guide patrons to safety. This includes ensuring that exits are properly used, identifying and addressing bottlenecks in evacuation routes, and managing large crowds under stressful conditions.

Nightclubs must also have clear fire evacuation plans in place, including maps of all exits and fire safety equipment. Security personnel should be fully familiar with these plans and be able to implement them at a moment's notice in the event of a fire.

Conclusion

Emergency procedures are a critical component of nightclub security. Staff must be trained in evacuation protocols to guide patrons to safety during emergencies, whether they involve fires, medical incidents, or violent outbreaks. First aid and medical emergency training, including certification in CPR and AED use, equip security personnel to handle injuries and medical crises effectively. Fire safety measures, such as knowing how to prevent overcrowding near exits and using fire safety equipment, are essential for preventing and managing fires in a nightclub setting. By mastering these emergency procedures, nightclub security personnel can ensure a safer, more secure environment for everyone involved.

Surveillance and Monitoring

Surveillance and monitoring play a crucial role in nightclub security, providing the necessary tools to maintain safety, prevent incidents, and document activities for future reference. With the prevalence of large crowds, alcohol consumption, and the high-energy atmosphere of nightclubs, security personnel must remain vigilant at all times. Effective use of surveillance systems, recognizing suspicious behavior, and proper incident reporting are essential skills that security staff must master to ensure a safe environment for patrons and staff alike. This guide explores the best practices for nightclub surveillance and monitoring, focusing on the use of surveillance systems, recognizing suspicious behavior, and accurate incident reporting.

Use of Surveillance Systems

Surveillance systems, such as closed-circuit television (CCTV), are a cornerstone of nightclub security. These systems provide a constant watch over various areas of the venue, enabling security staff to monitor activity in real time and respond quickly to potential threats or issues. Proper training in using surveillance systems is essential for security personnel to ensure maximum effectiveness in monitoring and documenting incidents.

1. Effective Use of CCTV

CCTV systems are one of the most commonly used surveillance tools in nightclubs. They provide an extra set of eyes, allowing security personnel to monitor multiple areas simultaneously, including entry points, dance floors, bar areas, VIP sections, and parking lots. By having a comprehensive view of the nightclub, CCTV helps security staff identify suspicious behavior, prevent altercations, and document incidents.

Training security personnel in the proper use of CCTV is critical. Staff should be familiar with the system's controls, such as how to zoom in on specific areas, adjust camera angles, and record footage. This ensures that important details, such as identifying individuals involved in altercations or thefts, are captured accurately.

In addition, security personnel must know how to use CCTV footage in real time to coordinate responses. For example, if a fight breaks out on the dance floor, staff monitoring the cameras can direct nearby security personnel to the exact location of the altercation, speeding up the response and minimizing the risk of injury to patrons.

2. Monitoring High-Risk Areas

Nightclubs often have specific areas where incidents are more likely to occur, such as entrances, exits, bars, restrooms, and VIP sections. These areas should be prioritized for surveillance, as they are common hotspots for conflicts, thefts, or drug activity. Cameras should be positioned to cover these areas effectively, with security personnel regularly reviewing the footage to ensure no suspicious activity goes unnoticed.

For instance, the entrance and exit areas should be closely monitored for signs of intoxicated or aggressive individuals entering or leaving the venue. The bar area, where patrons often consume alcohol, should also be watched for signs of over-intoxication or verbal disputes that could escalate into physical confrontations. Similarly, restrooms are areas where illegal drug use or altercations can occur, making them another key focus for surveillance.

3. Integration with Other Security Measures

Surveillance systems should not be viewed in isolation but rather as part of a comprehensive security strategy. For maximum effectiveness, CCTV systems should be integrated with other security tools and protocols. For example, surveillance systems can work alongside access control systems to monitor who is entering restricted areas, such as VIP sections or backstage zones. Security staff should use CCTV in coordination with communication devices, such as radios, to quickly relay information and dispatch personnel to respond to potential issues.

By leveraging surveillance systems as part of an overall security plan, nightclubs can significantly reduce the likelihood of incidents and ensure that their staff are better equipped to respond quickly and appropriately.

Recognizing Suspicious Behavior

Surveillance is only effective if security personnel are trained to recognize and interpret suspicious behavior. Identifying potential threats early allows security teams to intervene before problems escalate. Nightclub security staff must be able to spot warning signs that may indicate criminal activity, such as theft, drug use, or the presence of weapons, and take appropriate action to mitigate these risks.

1. Signs of Theft or Pickpocketing

Nightclubs are often crowded environments, making them attractive targets for thieves or pickpockets. Security personnel should be trained to recognize suspicious behavior associated with theft, such as individuals who are:

- Frequently bumping into others or standing unusually close to patrons.

- Distracting patrons while accomplices attempt to steal wallets, phones, or other valuables.

- Hovering around unattended bags or jackets, especially near coat-check areas.

Surveillance systems can help detect these behaviors, allowing security personnel to intervene before a theft occurs. In some cases, monitoring footage after an incident can also help identify suspects and recover stolen items.

2. Recognizing Illegal Drug Activity

Drug use and distribution are common concerns in nightclubs, and security personnel must be trained to recognize behaviors that suggest illegal drug activity. This might include patrons who are:

- Frequently retreating to secluded areas, such as restrooms or dark corners, to engage in suspicious transactions.

- Displaying erratic behavior or excessive intoxication that goes beyond typical alcohol consumption.

- Interacting with specific individuals multiple times in a short period, potentially indicating drug dealing.

By monitoring for these behaviors, security staff can prevent drug-related incidents and maintain a safer environment for patrons.

3. Identifying Potentially Dangerous Individuals

The presence of weapons or aggressive individuals in a nightclub is a serious threat to the safety of patrons and staff. Security personnel must be vigilant in spotting signs that someone may be carrying a weapon or preparing to engage in violent behavior. Indicators might include:

- Individuals repeatedly adjusting their clothing or bags in ways that suggest they are concealing a weapon.

- Patrons displaying aggressive body language, such as clenched fists, rapid pacing, or aggressive posturing.

- People who are constantly scanning the crowd or acting nervously, which could indicate they are planning an altercation or illegal activity.

Once suspicious behavior is identified, security staff should take steps to intervene quickly and safely. This might involve discreetly monitoring the individual for further signs, notifying team members, or directly confronting the patron, depending on the severity of the situation.

Incident Reporting

Accurate and thorough incident reporting is essential for documenting any events that occur within a nightclub, such as fights, accidents, or violations of club policies. Well-written reports serve as a legal record, provide valuable information for investigations, and help nightclub management make informed decisions about security improvements. Security personnel must be trained in how to document incidents clearly and comprehensively.

1. The Importance of Detailed Reports

Incident reports are important for several reasons. First, they provide a clear, objective record of what occurred during an incident, which can be useful for legal purposes. For example, if a fight breaks out and legal action is taken by one or more of the involved parties, a detailed incident report can serve as crucial evidence.

Second, reports help nightclub management and security teams analyze patterns in incidents. This allows the venue to adjust its security measures to prevent similar incidents in the future. For example, if reports frequently mention altercations in a specific area of the club, additional security personnel or surveillance may be assigned to that area.

2. Key Elements of an Incident Report

A comprehensive incident report should include the following elements:

- Date, time, and location: When and where the incident took place.

- Individuals involved: Names (if known), descriptions, and any identification details of the parties involved in the incident.

- Description of the incident: A clear and objective account of what occurred, including the actions taken by security personnel and any patrons involved.

- Witness statements: Testimonies from bystanders or other patrons who witnessed the incident can provide additional context or clarify details.

- Actions taken: Security staff should document the steps they took to resolve the situation, such as escorting individuals from the premises or contacting law enforcement.

- Evidence: If relevant, the report should include details about any physical evidence, such as security footage or items confiscated from patrons.

3. Consistency and Objectivity in Reporting

It is critical that incident reports are consistent and objective. Security personnel should avoid inserting personal opinions or assumptions into the report and instead focus on documenting the facts as they occurred. For example, rather than saying, "The patron was drunk and belligerent," the report should state, "The patron exhibited signs of intoxication, such as slurred speech and unsteady walking, and raised their voice in a verbal altercation."

Training staff to write clear, detailed, and unbiased reports ensures that incident documentation can withstand scrutiny in legal settings and provides accurate information for internal reviews.

Conclusion

Surveillance and monitoring are essential components of nightclub security. By training security personnel to effectively use surveillance systems, recognize suspicious behavior, and accurately document incidents, nightclubs can create a safer and more secure environment for patrons. Surveillance systems like CCTV provide critical oversight, while the ability to identify early signs of theft, drug activity, or aggression allows security to intervene before incidents escalate. Accurate incident reporting not only supports legal and investigative processes but also helps nightclubs improve their security protocols over time. When combined, these surveillance and monitoring techniques help ensure the safety and success of any nightlife venue.

Cultural Sensitivity and Inclusivity

In the modern nightclub environment, cultural sensitivity and inclusivity are essential components of effective security operations. Nightclubs attract a diverse array of patrons, coming from various racial, ethnic, gender, and socio-economic backgrounds. Additionally, nightclubs often serve as social hubs for LGBTQ+ communities and individuals of differing lifestyles. This diversity enriches the nightclub experience but also presents unique challenges for security personnel. Proper training in cultural sensitivity and inclusivity ensures that all patrons feel welcome, safe, and respected, regardless of their background.

Security personnel must be trained to understand, appreciate, and respect the diversity of the clientele they interact with daily. This training involves fostering an environment of inclusivity and addressing implicit biases to ensure that all interactions are conducted professionally and equitably. This guide will explore the importance of diversity training, bias awareness, and practical strategies for implementing cultural sensitivity and inclusivity in nightclub security.

Diversity Training

Diversity training is a critical first step toward creating an inclusive and respectful environment for all patrons. Security personnel must understand the importance of treating every individual with dignity, regardless of race, gender, sexual orientation, cultural background, or other differences. By promoting awareness and understanding of diverse experiences, diversity training helps foster empathy, reduce discrimination, and improve the overall nightclub atmosphere.

1. The Importance of Diversity Training

Nightclubs are vibrant social spaces where people of all backgrounds come together to relax, have fun, and express themselves. For many, nightclubs serve as important spaces for identity exploration and community building, particularly for marginalized groups such as LGBTQ+ individuals and people of color. Security personnel play a key role in ensuring that these spaces remain inclusive and welcoming by interacting with patrons fairly and respectfully.

Diversity training helps security staff develop the cultural competence necessary to navigate these interactions. This training not only benefits patrons but also strengthens the nightclub's reputation as a safe and inclusive venue. A welcoming environment attracts a broader and more diverse clientele, contributing to the success and sustainability of the business.

2. Components of Effective Diversity Training

An effective diversity training program should cover several key areas, including:

- Understanding cultural differences: Security personnel must be taught to recognize and respect cultural differences in communication, behavior, and personal space. For example, in some cultures, direct eye contact is a sign of confidence, while in others, it may be considered confrontational. By learning about these nuances, security staff can better interpret the actions and intentions of patrons from different backgrounds.

- Gender and sexual orientation awareness: Nightclubs often serve as safe spaces for members of the LGBTQ+ community. Security personnel must be trained to understand issues of gender identity and sexual orientation and to interact respectfully with patrons across the gender and sexuality spectrum. This includes using correct pronouns, avoiding assumptions about someone's gender or relationship status, and respecting non-binary or transgender individuals' experiences.

- Dealing with discrimination and harassment: Security staff must know how to handle situations involving discrimination or harassment, whether it is racially motivated, homophobic, or sexist in nature. Nightclubs are meant to be places of enjoyment, and any form of discrimination can create an unsafe and hostile environment. Security personnel must be proactive in addressing these issues and intervening if they witness any form of discrimination or harassment.

3. Creating Inclusive Policies

In addition to diversity training, nightclub management must establish clear policies that reflect a commitment to inclusivity. These policies should outline the club's stance against discrimination and harassment and provide guidelines for how staff should handle situations where patrons feel unsafe or marginalized.

For example, the club may implement a zero-tolerance policy for hate speech, racial slurs, or homophobic comments. Security staff should be trained to enforce these policies consistently and fairly. This can involve warning patrons who engage in inappropriate behavior, removing individuals from the premises if necessary, or contacting law enforcement in more serious cases.

Bias Awareness

Bias, whether conscious or unconscious, can significantly impact how security personnel interact with patrons. Security staff must be aware of their own biases and take steps to ensure that these biases do not affect their decision-making or treatment of guests. By promoting bias awareness, nightclub security teams can foster a more inclusive and equitable environment for all patrons.

1. Understanding Implicit Bias

Implicit bias refers to the unconscious attitudes or stereotypes that individuals hold toward certain groups of people. These biases can influence behavior in subtle ways, often without the person even realizing it. For example, a security guard may unconsciously assume that certain patrons are more likely to cause trouble based on their appearance, race, or manner of dress, even if there is no evidence to support this assumption.

Implicit biases can lead to unequal treatment of patrons, whether through overly harsh enforcement of rules, disproportionately targeting certain groups for searches or scrutiny, or making assumptions about a person's behavior based on stereotypes. This type of biased behavior can create an unwelcoming and discriminatory atmosphere, making patrons feel targeted or unsafe.

Security personnel must be trained to recognize their own biases and work actively to overcome them. Training programs can include exercises that help staff identify common stereotypes and learn strategies for mitigating their impact on decision-making.

2. Treating Patrons Equitably

One of the key goals of bias awareness training is to ensure that all patrons are treated equitably. This means applying the same standards and rules to everyone, regardless of their background, appearance, or identity. Security personnel should be consistent in their enforcement of nightclub policies, such as dress codes, behavior standards, and alcohol consumption limits.

Bias can sometimes manifest in small, everyday decisions, such as who gets searched more thoroughly at the door or who is approached more quickly for potentially inappropriate behavior. By being conscious of these decisions and ensuring that they are based on actions rather than assumptions, security staff can create a more equitable and inclusive environment.

3. Handling Bias-Related Incidents

Unfortunately, bias-related incidents can occur both among patrons and, at times, among staff members. It is essential that security personnel are prepared to handle these incidents professionally and fairly. If a patron feels they have been discriminated against by another guest or by security staff, the situation must be addressed promptly and respectfully.

Security staff should be trained to listen carefully to the concerns of patrons who feel targeted or uncomfortable. This includes offering a safe space for individuals to express their concerns and investigating the situation thoroughly. If the bias-related behavior comes from another patron, appropriate action should be taken, such as issuing a warning, removing the offending individual, or contacting law enforcement if necessary.

Promoting an Inclusive Environment

Beyond formal training and policies, promoting an inclusive environment is an ongoing effort that requires attention to detail and commitment from nightclub management and security personnel alike. Some practical strategies include:

- Inclusive Language: Security staff should use inclusive language when addressing patrons. This includes using gender-neutral language when appropriate and avoiding assumptions about a person's gender, pronouns, or identity. Training staff to ask for preferred pronouns respectfully and use them correctly can help ensure all patrons feel respected.

- Visibility of Inclusivity Policies: Posting clear signage at entrances and throughout the club that states the venue's commitment to inclusivity and its policies on discrimination can set the tone for patrons. This can include signs indicating that hate speech, harassment, and discrimination are not tolerated.

- Creating Safe Spaces: For venues that serve diverse communities, creating designated safe spaces or areas where marginalized groups can feel comfortable can enhance the sense of inclusivity. For example, LGBTQ+ patrons may feel safer if there are designated areas that are clearly inclusive and welcoming, and security personnel assigned to these areas should receive specialized training to ensure they understand the community's needs.

- Hiring Diverse Staff: Ensuring diversity within the security team itself can foster a greater sense of inclusion. Diverse teams bring a wider range of perspectives, experiences, and cultural competencies, which can help the staff relate to a broader range of patrons.

Conclusion

Cultural sensitivity and inclusivity are essential aspects of nightclub security. Through diversity training and bias awareness, security personnel can ensure that all patrons, regardless of their race, gender, sexual orientation, or cultural background, feel welcome and respected. These efforts not only create a safer environment but also contribute to the long-term success and reputation of the nightclub as an inclusive and welcoming space. By implementing clear policies, promoting equity in treatment, and actively addressing incidents of discrimination or bias, nightclub security staff can help foster an environment where all patrons feel safe and valued.

Handling VIP and High-Profile Guests

Managing security for VIP and high-profile guests in nightclubs is a specialized task that requires discretion, professionalism, and an elevated level of attention to detail. These guests, often celebrities, influencers, or high-net-worth individuals, expect privacy and protection without feeling overwhelmed by overt security measures. The challenge for nightclub security personnel is to ensure that these individuals feel safe and comfortable while minimizing disruption to the overall environment. This involves balancing effective protection with a discreet presence, managing access to VIP areas, and interacting professionally with high-profile guests.

Security personnel must be thoroughly trained in the specific protocols and nuances involved in handling VIP guests, including how to manage VIP areas, maintain professionalism around celebrities, and address potential threats or disturbances in these exclusive sections.

Special Protocols for VIP Areas

VIP areas in nightclubs are designated sections reserved for celebrities, high-profile individuals, or patrons willing to pay a premium for an exclusive experience. These areas typically offer enhanced privacy and personalized service, making them attractive spaces for those seeking to enjoy the nightclub atmosphere away from the general crowd. However, managing these spaces presents unique security challenges. Security personnel must be well-versed in controlling access to these areas, maintaining the privacy of guests, and addressing any potential disturbances quickly and effectively.

1. Controlling Access to VIP Sections

One of the most critical aspects of handling VIP security is ensuring that access to VIP areas is tightly controlled. Security personnel must be trained to verify the identity of individuals who are allowed into these sections and to prevent unauthorized access. This involves managing guest lists, checking wristbands or other forms of identification, and ensuring that only those with the appropriate credentials are permitted entry.

Security staff should also be aware of any special arrangements made for specific guests, such as friends or associates of the VIP who may not be on the official guest list but have been granted access by the venue's management. Clear communication between the security team and nightclub management is essential to avoid confusion or confrontations at the entrance to VIP areas.

2. Monitoring VIP Sections for Potential Threats

Once inside the VIP area, security personnel must be vigilant in monitoring for potential threats or disturbances. While these sections are often separated from the general crowd, they are not immune to the same risks that can arise in the rest of the nightclub, including intoxicated patrons, aggressive behavior, or unwanted attention from other guests.

Security staff should remain discreet but attentive, keeping an eye on interactions within the VIP area to prevent potential issues before they escalate. For example, if a guest from the general crowd attempts to approach a high-profile individual, security should intervene politely but firmly to prevent any intrusion on the VIP's privacy. Similarly, security personnel must be prepared to respond quickly to any signs of aggression or inappropriate behavior, ensuring that the VIP section remains a safe and enjoyable space.

3. Handling Disturbances in VIP Areas

Disturbances in VIP sections can be particularly sensitive, as high-profile guests may be more concerned about maintaining their privacy and avoiding negative publicity. Security personnel must be trained to handle any issues with discretion, professionalism, and minimal disruption.

If a disturbance arises, such as a disagreement between guests or an intoxicated individual causing a scene, security should de-escalate the situation quickly and quietly. The goal is to resolve the issue without drawing unnecessary attention or causing embarrassment to the VIP guests. This may involve escorting disruptive individuals out of the VIP area or, in more severe cases, removing them from the nightclub entirely.

Professionalism Around High-Profile Guests

When working in close proximity to high-profile guests, such as celebrities, influencers, or public figures, security personnel must maintain a high level of professionalism at all times. These individuals often value their privacy and are used to receiving special attention. However, they do not want to feel overwhelmed or constantly under scrutiny. Security staff must strike a balance between providing protection and allowing these guests to enjoy their experience without feeling like they are under constant surveillance.

1. Ensuring Privacy and Discretion

The privacy of high-profile guests is of utmost importance. Many celebrities and VIPs visit nightclubs to relax and enjoy themselves without being subjected to public scrutiny or unwanted attention. Security personnel must respect this desire for privacy by maintaining a low profile and avoiding unnecessary interactions with VIP guests unless their safety is at risk.

For example, security staff should avoid engaging in casual conversation with high-profile individuals unless approached, and they should never ask for autographs, photos, or personal favors. Additionally, any incidents or security concerns involving VIP guests should be handled discreetly, without drawing the attention of other patrons or media outlets.

VIP guests will appreciate security staff who can blend into the background while remaining vigilant, ensuring that their night is both safe and private.

2. Maintaining Professional Boundaries

It's important for security personnel to maintain clear professional boundaries when working around high-profile guests. This means avoiding overly familiar or casual behavior and always treating the VIP with respect. Security staff should be polite and courteous, but never intrusive.

In situations where a VIP guest requests assistance, such as help with crowd control, arranging transportation, or resolving issues with other patrons, security personnel should respond promptly and professionally. Any requests should be handled efficiently, without causing undue disruption to the guest's experience.

By maintaining these professional boundaries, security staff can build trust with high-profile guests, ensuring that they feel secure and respected throughout their time at the nightclub.

3. Managing Public and Media Attention

High-profile individuals often attract the attention of the public and the media. In a nightclub setting, this can lead to unwanted attention from other patrons, photographers, or even paparazzi outside the venue. Security personnel must be prepared to manage these situations with tact and professionalism.

If a VIP guest is being harassed by patrons seeking autographs or photos, security staff should intervene politely but firmly, reminding patrons to respect the guest's privacy. In cases where paparazzi or photographers attempt to take intrusive photos, security personnel should work with nightclub management to establish clear guidelines regarding photography and ensure that these rules are enforced consistently.

It is also important for security personnel to coordinate with the VIP's personal security team, if applicable. Many high-profile guests travel with their own bodyguards or security detail, and nightclub security should work collaboratively with these teams to provide seamless protection. Clear communication and coordination between the nightclub security staff and the VIP's personal security team can help prevent any security gaps or misunderstandings.

Handling Potential Threats

In addition to managing access and maintaining professionalism, nightclub security personnel must be prepared to address any potential threats to the safety of high-profile guests. VIPs are often targeted by overzealous fans, opportunistic individuals, or even those with malicious intent. As such, security staff must be trained to identify and mitigate potential threats quickly and effectively.

1. Identifying Unwanted Attention

One of the most common threats to high-profile guests in a nightclub setting is unwanted attention from other patrons. While many fans may approach celebrities or VIPs out of genuine admiration, these interactions can quickly become overwhelming or inappropriate, especially if alcohol is involved.

Security personnel must be alert to any patrons attempting to engage with VIP guests in ways that make them uncomfortable. This may include persistent requests for photos, autographs, or personal interactions, as well as more aggressive behavior such as touching or following the guest. In these situations, security should intervene promptly, guiding the patron away from the VIP area while remaining polite and respectful.

2. Preventing Physical Threats

In more serious cases, high-profile guests may face physical threats, whether from aggressive patrons or individuals attempting to cause harm. Security personnel must be trained to recognize early warning signs of aggressive behavior and take immediate action to protect the VIP guest.

This may involve positioning security staff strategically around the VIP section to monitor for suspicious behavior, conducting thorough checks of individuals attempting to enter the VIP area, and coordinating with the VIP's personal security team if necessary. In the event of a physical threat, security staff must act quickly to escort the VIP guest to a safe location while neutralizing the threat.

Conclusion

Handling VIP and high-profile guests in nightclubs requires a combination of discretion, professionalism, and preparedness. By implementing special protocols for VIP areas, maintaining a high level of professionalism around celebrities, and addressing potential threats swiftly and discreetly, security personnel can ensure that these individuals enjoy their time at the nightclub in safety and comfort. Proper training in these areas helps create a secure and welcoming environment for VIPs, enhancing the nightclub's reputation as a venue that caters to high-profile guests with care and respect.

Post-Incident Management

Post-incident management is a crucial aspect of nightclub security. How an incident is handled after it occurs can have significant implications for the safety of patrons, the legal standing of the nightclub, and the security personnel themselves. Effective post-incident management involves meticulous documentation, cooperation with law enforcement, and an understanding of the potential legal consequences that may arise from incidents. Security personnel must be trained to respond professionally and efficiently in the aftermath of incidents, ensuring that they protect the nightclub's interests while also complying with legal and ethical standards.

This guide explores the key components of post-incident management, focusing on proper incident documentation, cooperation with law enforcement, and the legal aftermath of incidents.

Incident Documentation

Clear and detailed incident documentation is essential for several reasons. It provides an official record of what occurred, helps the nightclub management address potential risks or legal liabilities, and supports law enforcement investigations or legal proceedings if necessary. Security personnel must be trained in writing thorough, factual, and objective incident reports that capture all relevant details.

1. The Importance of Accurate Documentation

Incident reports serve multiple purposes. First, they provide a factual account of what happened during an incident, which can be crucial for legal proceedings or insurance claims. For example, if a fight breaks out in the nightclub and someone is injured, the incident report can serve as evidence in any potential lawsuits or criminal charges that follow.

Second, incident documentation helps nightclub management identify and address safety concerns. By reviewing incident reports, management can spot patterns of behavior that may require intervention, such as increasing security in certain areas of the venue or refining policies related to alcohol service or crowd control.

Finally, detailed documentation helps protect security personnel themselves. If a security guard's actions during an incident are later questioned, a well-written report provides a clear account of the decisions made and why they were necessary.

2. Writing Clear, Factual, and Detailed Reports

When documenting incidents, security personnel should aim for clarity, objectivity, and thoroughness. An incident report should answer the basic questions of who, what, where, when, why, and how. Here are the key elements that should be included in any incident report:

- Date, time, and location: When and where the incident occurred.

- Names and descriptions: Full names, descriptions, or identifying details of individuals involved in the incident, including witnesses if available.

- Sequence of events: A clear, chronological account of what happened leading up to the incident, during the event, and after the incident was resolved.

- Actions taken: A detailed description of the actions taken by security staff to address the situation, including de-escalation efforts, physical interventions, or any communications with other staff or law enforcement.

- Injuries or damages: Documentation of any injuries sustained or property damage that occurred as a result of the incident.

- Evidence: Notes on any physical evidence collected, such as video footage, witness statements, or items involved in the incident.

It is essential to avoid inserting personal opinions, assumptions, or speculation into the report. The goal is to provide an accurate, objective account of the facts as they occurred. For example, rather than stating, "The patron was clearly intoxicated and causing trouble," the report should say, "The patron appeared to be intoxicated, based on slurred speech and unsteady movement, and was involved in a verbal altercation with another individual."

Training in report writing is critical for ensuring that all security personnel are capable of producing professional, detailed incident reports that hold up under legal scrutiny.

Cooperating with Law Enforcement

In many cases, incidents in a nightclub setting may require the involvement of law enforcement. Whether it's a physical altercation, a medical emergency, or criminal activity such as drug use or theft, security personnel must be prepared to cooperate fully with police or other authorities. This cooperation includes securing crime scenes, preserving evidence, and providing accurate witness statements.

1. Securing the Crime Scene

If an incident involves a potential crime, such as an assault or theft, one of the first responsibilities of security personnel is to secure the area where the incident occurred. This means preventing unauthorized individuals from entering the scene and potentially contaminating evidence. Security staff should cordon off the area and ensure that no one interferes with physical evidence, such as weapons, personal belongings, or damaged property.

Securing the crime scene also involves monitoring individuals who may be involved in the incident to ensure they do not leave the premises before law enforcement arrives. If someone attempts to flee, security personnel should notify the police immediately, providing a description and any other relevant details.

2. Preserving Evidence

In addition to securing the scene, preserving evidence is a critical responsibility for nightclub security. Evidence may include physical items (such as clothing, weapons, or stolen property), surveillance footage, or witness statements. Security personnel must take steps to ensure that evidence is not tampered with, destroyed, or removed before law enforcement can examine it.

For instance, if a fight breaks out and a weapon is used, security should make sure the weapon is not handled or moved. Instead, the area should be secured, and the weapon should be left in place for law enforcement to collect. Additionally, if the incident was captured on CCTV, security personnel should immediately preserve the footage and provide it to police upon request.

3. Providing Witness Statements

Security personnel are often key witnesses to incidents that occur in the nightclub, and their statements can be vital to law enforcement investigations. When giving a statement, security staff should be clear, factual, and consistent with the incident report they have written. They should avoid speculating or offering opinions about what may have occurred; instead, they should focus on recounting the facts as they witnessed them.

It is also important for security personnel to cooperate fully with any follow-up requests from law enforcement. This may include providing additional documentation, participating in interviews, or testifying in court if necessary.

Legal Aftermath

The legal consequences of incidents that occur in nightclubs can be significant, both for the venue itself and for the security personnel involved. Understanding the potential legal ramifications is essential for security staff, as their actions (or inactions) during an incident can impact the nightclub's liability and their own legal standing. Proper post-incident management helps mitigate these risks by ensuring that security staff follow best practices in documentation, cooperation with law enforcement, and adherence to legal protocols.

1. Potential Legal Consequences for the Nightclub

When incidents occur in a nightclub, there is always the potential for legal action to be taken by the individuals involved. For example, if a patron is injured in a fight or due to a slip and fall, they may file a lawsuit against the nightclub, claiming negligence. Similarly, if a patron is ejected from the premises and claims they were assaulted by security personnel, the nightclub could face legal challenges related to excessive force.

To minimize the nightclub's legal exposure, it is crucial that security staff follow all protocols for post-incident management. Proper documentation, preserving evidence, and cooperating with law enforcement all play a role in protecting the nightclub from liability.

2. Legal Risks for Security Personnel

Security personnel themselves may also face legal consequences following an incident, especially if their actions are called into question. For example, if a security guard uses excessive force while removing a patron from the venue, they could be subject to criminal charges or civil lawsuits. In such cases, the quality of the incident report and any witness statements can be critical in determining whether the guard's actions were justified.

Security staff should also be aware that failing to act in certain situations can have legal repercussions. For instance, if security personnel witness a violent altercation but fail to intervene appropriately, they could be held liable for failing to prevent further harm.

3. Understanding Role in Lawsuits or Criminal Proceedings

In some instances, security personnel may be called to testify in court, either as part of a civil lawsuit or a criminal proceeding. This could involve recounting their observations, explaining the actions they took during the incident, or providing additional evidence such as surveillance footage or incident reports.

It is important for security staff to remain professional and factual when involved in any legal proceedings. They should review their incident reports and any relevant documentation beforehand to ensure consistency in their testimony. Additionally, they should avoid embellishing details or providing information that is not directly relevant to the case.

Conclusion

Post-incident management is a vital part of nightclub security operations. Proper incident documentation, cooperation with law enforcement, and an understanding of the legal aftermath of incidents are essential for protecting both the nightclub and its security personnel. By training staff to handle incidents professionally and efficiently, nightclubs can reduce legal risks, improve safety outcomes, and ensure that their security teams are prepared to address any challenges that arise in the aftermath of an incident.

Ongoing Training and Drills

Effective nightclub security requires more than just basic training; it demands ongoing education, skills refreshers, and regular drills to ensure that security personnel remain prepared for the dynamic challenges they face. Nightclub environments are fast-paced, and unpredictable situations can arise at any moment, making it critical for security teams to stay sharp, adaptable, and ready to act quickly. Regular training ensures that personnel are not only equipped with the latest techniques in conflict resolution and crisis management but are also able to maintain high levels of professionalism and legal compliance.

This guide explores the importance of regular refresher training, the value of conducting simulation exercises, and how both contribute to building a well-prepared and effective nightclub security team.

Regular Refreshers

Security training should not be a one-time event but rather an ongoing process that ensures personnel are constantly improving and maintaining their skills. Nightclubs are environments where risks and security challenges can evolve quickly, from shifts in patron behavior to new safety regulations. To address these challenges, regular refresher training is essential.

1. Keeping Skills Sharp

Ongoing refresher training ensures that security personnel retain and refine the skills they need to manage the nightclub environment. This includes the full range of competencies, from interpersonal communication and de-escalation techniques to physical intervention skills and legal knowledge. Even highly experienced security personnel benefit from regular practice and reminders of best practices.

For example, a security guard who has received de-escalation training early in their career may need periodic refreshers to ensure that they continue to use the most effective techniques when handling confrontational patrons. These refreshers can help reinforce the importance of using calm, clear communication and non-physical methods to resolve conflicts, ultimately reducing the likelihood of violence or injury.

2. Staying Updated on Legal and Procedural Changes

Nightclub security is often governed by evolving legal requirements and safety regulations. For instance, changes in local laws regarding the use of force, alcohol service, or crowd management may affect how security personnel conduct their duties. Regular training sessions provide an opportunity for security staff to stay informed about these changes and adapt their practices accordingly.

Additionally, management may implement new internal policies or protocols based on past incidents or shifting priorities, such as increased focus on preventing drug activity or managing large events. By providing regular refreshers, nightclubs can ensure that all staff are aware of these updates and are prepared to follow them in real-time situations.

3. Reinforcing Emergency Procedures

In any emergency, the ability to respond quickly and correctly is crucial. Regular drills and refresher training in emergency procedures, such as fire evacuations, medical crises, or violent incidents, help ensure that security personnel can respond effectively when a real emergency arises. Familiarity with exit routes, fire suppression equipment, and first aid techniques must be maintained through consistent practice.

Periodic training sessions that revisit these key procedures reinforce muscle memory, so security staff can act swiftly under pressure. For example, fire drills help security personnel remember the most efficient evacuation routes and how to guide patrons safely to exits, even when the environment is chaotic.

Simulations

In addition to regular classroom-style training or discussions, practical, hands-on simulation exercises are essential for preparing nightclub security teams for high-risk scenarios. Simulations provide a safe, controlled environment where security personnel can practice responding to a range of challenging situations that they may encounter in real life.

1. Active Shooter Scenarios

While rare, the possibility of an active shooter situation is one of the most dangerous threats a nightclub could face. Security personnel must be trained to respond swiftly and appropriately, ensuring the safety of patrons and staff. Conducting active shooter simulations can help security teams practice critical actions such as:

- Identifying threats quickly: In a real situation, the ability to rapidly identify the source of danger can be life-saving. Simulations provide an opportunity to practice this skill in a controlled environment.

- Coordinating with law enforcement: Security personnel must know how to communicate effectively with law enforcement, provide accurate information about the location and nature of the threat, and assist with crowd control while first responders address the situation.

- Executing evacuation or lockdown procedures: Depending on the scenario, security may need to either evacuate patrons or instruct them to shelter in place. Active shooter simulations help staff become familiar with both approaches and understand when each is appropriate.

Regular simulations of high-risk scenarios help nightclub security personnel internalize the steps they need to take in an emergency, reducing hesitation and ensuring that they can respond quickly and effectively.

2. Large Brawls and Crowd Control

Nightclubs can sometimes experience large fights or brawls, particularly in settings where alcohol is involved. Security personnel must be prepared to break up these fights quickly to prevent injury or property damage and to restore order in the venue. Simulating large brawls can provide security staff with valuable experience in handling physical altercations, crowd control, and conflict resolution under pressure.

Key elements of a brawl simulation might include:

- Coordinating with other security staff: Large brawls often require multiple security personnel to intervene at once. Simulations can help staff practice communicating with one another via radios or hand signals, working as a team to control the situation.

- Safely intervening in fights: Security personnel must know how to separate individuals involved in a fight without escalating the violence or causing additional harm. This can include training in safe physical restraint techniques and understanding when to call for backup.

- Calming surrounding crowds: Large altercations often draw attention from nearby patrons, and security must also manage the crowd's reaction. Simulations provide a chance to practice keeping bystanders away from the scene of the fight and ensuring that the area does not become a hotspot for further conflict.

3. Medical Emergencies

Medical emergencies are not uncommon in nightclub settings, where alcohol consumption and high-energy environments can lead to accidents, overdoses, or health crises. Security personnel must be prepared to provide first aid and manage the situation until professional medical help arrives.

Medical emergency simulations might cover:

- Administering first aid: Security staff should be trained in basic first aid, CPR, and the use of Automated External Defibrillators (AEDs). Simulating real medical emergencies allows personnel to practice these skills and become comfortable using the equipment.

- Overdose response: Given the prevalence of alcohol and drug use in nightlife settings, security teams must be trained to recognize the signs of alcohol poisoning or drug overdose and take appropriate action. Simulations can help staff practice responding calmly, providing care, and communicating effectively with medical responders.

- Managing the crowd during a medical emergency: When a medical emergency occurs in a crowded nightclub, security personnel must keep the area clear for first responders while ensuring that the situation does not create panic among other patrons.

Simulations create realistic conditions where security personnel can practice these responses without the pressure of a real-life emergency. By rehearsing various scenarios, security staff become more confident in their ability to manage high-risk situations.

Conclusion

Nightclub security requires a wide range of skills, from de-escalation and conflict resolution to crisis management and emergency response. Ongoing training and regular drills are essential for keeping security personnel prepared for the evolving challenges they may face on the job. By incorporating regular refresher courses and simulation exercises into their training programs, nightclubs can ensure that their security teams are equipped to handle a variety of scenarios, from routine conflicts to life-threatening emergencies.

Effective training focuses not only on prevention and de-escalation but also on preparing for the possibility of violence, large-scale incidents, or medical emergencies. Simulations provide hands-on experience in handling high-risk situations, reinforcing both technical skills and the ability to remain calm under pressure. Ongoing training fosters a culture of preparedness and professionalism within the security team, ensuring that they can provide a safe and enjoyable environment for all patrons. In the fast-paced and unpredictable world of nightclubs, this level of readiness is essential for the success of the venue and the safety of everyone involved.

Conclusion

Nightclub security is an indispensable part of ensuring the safety and well-being of patrons, staff, and performers within the lively, often unpredictable environment of nightlife venues. The role of nightclub security goes far beyond simply standing at the door or breaking up fights; it encompasses a wide array of responsibilities, from crowd control and access management to conflict resolution, legal compliance, and emergency response. Effective nightclub security requires a comprehensive understanding of the dynamics at play in such venues, as well as a blend of interpersonal, legal, and physical skills to maintain a safe and enjoyable atmosphere for all.

Creating a Safe and Enjoyable Environment

At the core of nightclub security is the responsibility to create a safe and enjoyable space for patrons. This involves ensuring that people can relax, dance, and socialize without fear of harm or disruption. By proactively managing crowds, identifying potential threats early, and handling issues such as intoxicated patrons or conflicts before they escalate, security personnel play a vital role in maintaining a positive experience for everyone in the venue.

The ability to anticipate and mitigate risks is crucial for ensuring that problems are dealt with quickly and quietly. Whether it's controlling access at the door, managing VIP areas, or monitoring the crowd for signs of trouble, nightclub security staff must stay vigilant and responsive to the needs of the environment. A well-trained security team helps prevent problems from arising and responds swiftly when they do, maintaining order while ensuring that patrons feel safe and respected.

The Role of Interpersonal Skills

A significant aspect of nightclub security involves interacting with a wide variety of people, often under challenging circumstances. Nightclubs attract a diverse crowd, and security personnel must be adept at communicating with individuals from different backgrounds, cultures, and levels of intoxication. The ability to handle these interactions with professionalism, empathy, and respect is a critical skill that goes a long way in preventing conflicts and maintaining order.

Conflict resolution and de-escalation techniques are essential tools for nightclub security teams. Rather than relying solely on physical intervention, security staff should be trained to use verbal de-escalation strategies to diffuse tense situations before they become physical. This not only reduces the risk of injury to both patrons and staff but also helps create an environment where people feel comfortable and safe. The ability to stay calm, communicate clearly, and maintain control without aggression is a hallmark of effective nightclub security.

Legal Knowledge and Compliance

Understanding the legal framework that governs nightclub security is also crucial. Security personnel must be familiar with local laws, particularly regarding the use of force, detainment of individuals, rights of refusal, and handling of minors or intoxicated patrons. Legal knowledge ensures that security actions are compliant with the law, reducing the risk of legal liability for the nightclub and its staff.

Additionally, security personnel must be trained in how to document incidents properly. Clear, factual incident reports are essential for protecting the nightclub in case of legal disputes and for cooperating with law enforcement when necessary. Whether an incident involves a fight, theft, or medical emergency, accurate documentation ensures that all relevant details are recorded and can be used in any subsequent legal proceedings.

Licensing and compliance with local regulations, such as fire codes, alcohol service laws, and security training requirements, further underline the importance of legal knowledge. By staying informed about these requirements and regularly updating their training, security teams can ensure that they operate within the bounds of the law, keeping the nightclub in good standing with authorities.

Emergency Preparedness

Nightclub security teams must be ready to handle a wide range of emergencies, from fires and medical incidents to violent outbreaks. Being prepared for these scenarios involves not only understanding how to respond but also conducting regular drills and training to ensure that the entire team can act quickly and effectively in an emergency. Proper evacuation protocols, first aid training, and knowledge of fire safety procedures are essential components of a security team's responsibilities.

In the event of a medical emergency, such as an overdose or injury, security personnel must be able to provide immediate care, including administering CPR or using an Automated External Defibrillator (AED) until professional medical help arrives. Regular training in these life-saving techniques is crucial for minimizing the impact of medical crises within the nightclub.

The Importance of Ongoing Training

Nightclub security is not a static field, and ongoing training is essential for keeping staff prepared for new challenges. Regular refresher courses and simulation exercises ensure that security personnel remain proficient in handling a variety of situations, from conflict resolution to emergency response. Simulations of high-risk scenarios, such as large brawls, active shooter situations, or medical emergencies, provide security staff with the hands-on experience they need to respond effectively in real-life situations.

By prioritizing ongoing education, nightclubs can ensure that their security teams are equipped to manage the evolving risks of the nightlife environment. Training should focus on both prevention and crisis management, helping security personnel to avoid incidents wherever possible and to respond swiftly and professionally when issues arise.

Final Thoughts

In conclusion, nightclub security is a multifaceted responsibility that requires a well-rounded skill set, including strong interpersonal abilities, legal knowledge, crisis management, and emergency preparedness. The safety and enjoyment of patrons, staff, and high-profile guests depend on the professionalism and effectiveness of the security team. Through ongoing training, legal compliance, and a focus on de-escalation and prevention, nightclub security personnel can create a secure and welcoming environment, ensuring that everyone has a positive experience. The blend of vigilance, empathy, and preparedness that defines effective nightclub security is what makes nightclubs not only safe but also enjoyable spaces for all who enter.

About the Author

Tom Sotis has been training consistently in various fighting methods since 1969. In addition to empty hands, weapons, and firearms skills, he is now well recognized as the leading edged weapons instructor in the world recognized for contributions to international and US federal agencies, for his specialized expertise in the use of weapons.

In addition to 50+ years of dedicated training in martial arts, combative methods, tactical knife fighting, and firearms, Tom gained practical street experience through decades of working in conflict-oriented professions.

In the early 1980's Tom began his career in the gang-warfare sections of Los Angeles, California. He was trained as a criminal investigator, undercover investigator, and fugitive recovery agent. Tom returned to New England and operated his own agency, Metro Criminal Investigations, for another ten years. He has many years of experience in nightclub integrity investigations and security.

Tom has traveled to 25 countries pioneering the forward evolution of edged weapons combat through extensive travel and research. Internationally, Tom's work experience includes, but is not limited to training: Cambodian Special Forces, Danish Law Enforcement, Hellenic (Greek) Coast Guard, Mexican Federal Police and Prison Guards, New Zealand Prison Guards, Norwegian Law Enforcement, Russian Spetsnaz and Criminal Investigation Units, South African Military, Police, and Security Forces, and Spanish Law Enforcement.

For over 30 years, Tom has worked with numerous US government agencies, specialist military teams, and various levels of law enforcement agencies. This list includes US

Intelligence Agencies, US Special Forces, US Secret Service/ERT, Federal Bureau of Investigation, Drug Enforcement Administration, the Internal Revenue Service, and the New England Organized Crime / Drug Enforcement Task Force.

On the state level, Tom has trained numerous State Police, SWAT, Defensive Tactics Instructors, Municipal Police Departments, County Sheriffs, and Corrections Special Response Teams. While he continues to train Law Enforcement Agencies, Tom serves on the Palm Beach Sheriff's Volunteer Marine Unit.

In the private sector, Tom trains Private Security Firms, Companies and Businesses, Firearms Groups, Combatives Groups, Martial arts organizations, High-risk groups, and Community groups.

An avid researcher on psychology and human performance, Tom became a certified Motivation Analyst licensed to administer and interpret the Reiss Motivation Profile®, the world's first scientifically validated and most accurate method of personality profiling and predicting behavior.

Tom Sotis LLC presently comprises three training companies: Truly Safer (Self-Protection), Amok Global (Use of Weapons) and Carry Safer (Defensive Shooting) as well as Performance Optimization Coaching, Motivational Profiling Analysis, and instructional videos on Tactical Knife Fighting and Unarmed Knife Defense.

Other books by Tom Sotis

Global Crime Syndicates

Bounty Hunters

Truly Safer

Sharp Strategies

The Way of Tactics

Unbreakable Honor

The Character Code

The Science of Motivation

Scientific Athletic Motivation

You are invited to visit his website
www.TomSotis.com
tom@tomsotis.com

www.ingramcontent.com/pod-product-compliance
Lightning Source LLC
Chambersburg PA
CBHW060419290526
45791CB00002B/822